LIKE WHEN YOU WAVE AT A TRAIN AND
THE TRAIN HOOTS BACK AT YOU

FARID'S BOOK

*other books by the author*

**Poetry:**
Dawn Visions
Burnt Heart/Ode to the War Dead
This Body of Black Light Gone Through the Diamond
The Desert is the Only Way Out
The Chronicles of Akhira
Halley's Comet
Awake as Never Before
The Ramadan Sonnets
The Blind Beekeeper
Mars & Beyond
Laughing Buddha Weeping Sufi
Salt Prayers
Ramadan Sonnets (The Ecstatic Exchange revised edition)
Psalms for the Brokenhearted
I Imagine a Lion
Coattails of the Saint
Abdallah Jones and the Disappearing-Dust Caper
Love is a Letter Burning in a High Wind
The Flame of Transformation Turns to Light
Underwater Galaxies
The Music Space
Cooked Oranges
Through Rose Colored Glasses
Like When You Wave at a Train and the Train Hoots Back at You

**Theater / The Floating Lotus Magic Opera Company:**
The Walls Are Running Blood
Bliss Apocalypse

**Puppet Theater:**
The Mystical Romance of Layla & Majnun
The Journey to Qalbiyya

**Compilation of Quotes:** Warrior Wisdom

**Prose:** Zen Rock Gardening
The Little Book of Zen
Zen Wisdom

# LIKE WHEN YOU WAVE AT A TRAIN AND THE TRAIN HOOTS BACK AT YOU

Farid's Book

poems

June 11 – July 26, November 6-9, 1991

Daniel Abdal-Hayy Moore

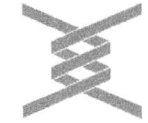

The Ecstatic Exchange
2008
Philadelphia

Like When You Wave at a Train and the Train Hoots Back at You / Farid's Book
Copyright © 2008 Daniel Abdal-Hayy Moore
All rights reserved.
Printed in the United States of America

For quotes any longer than those for critical articles and reviews, contact:
*The Ecstatic Exchange*,
6470 Morris Park Road, Philadelphia, PA 19151-2403
email: abdalhayy@danielmoorepoetry.com

First Edition
ISBN: 978-0-6152-0490-1 (paper)
Published by *The Ecstatic Exchange*,
6470 Morris Park Road, Philadelphia, PA 19151-2403

Also available from The Ecstatic Exchange:
*Knocking from Inside*, poems by Tiel Aisha Ansari

Cover and text design by Abdallateef Whiteman / www.ianwhiteman.com
Cover collage by the author
Back cover photos of author at Boy Scout Jamboree,
by unknown photographer, and today, by the author

DEDICATION

For Farid & Tina

on the occasion of their marriage

August 8, 2008

in Zurich, Switzerland

## CONTENTS

A Few Words of Introduction    8

| | | |
|---|---|---|
| 1 | White Eagle in a Pit | 13 |
| 2 | First Days | 15 |
| 3 | As for Us | 18 |
| 4 | Astronomical Reflector | 20 |
| 5 | I Want to Talk to You | 22 |
| 6 | Holes | 24 |
| 7 | Sage Advice | 26 |
| 8 | Ancestral Fathers | 28 |
| 9 | Sex | 30 |
| 10 | That Sound | 32 |
| 11 | That First Memory | 33 |
| 12 | At the Heart of the Atom | 35 |
| 13 | Actual Baseball | 38 |
| 14 | Supernatural Son | 40 |
| 15 | Limits | 41 |
| 16 | Woman | 43 |
| 17 | More Sage Advice | 45 |
| 18 | Legacy | 47 |
| 19 | The You in All This | 51 |
| 20 | Readiness for Death | 55 |

| | | |
|---|---|---|
| 21 | The Trouble Is | 58 |
| 22 | Happiness | 61 |
| 23 | Like When You Wave at a Train and the Train Hoots Back at You | 64 |
| 24 | To Weep Real Tears | 76 |
| 25 | The Father | 80 |
| 26 | The Son | 84 |
| | Prayer | 85 |

# A FEW WORDS OF INTRODUCTION

THIS MAY BE MY MOST personal book, as I wrote this collection of poems as an attempt to definitively and honestly connect in a deep way with Farid, my teenage stepson. The dynamic of our relationship, from the time of our entrance into each other's lives after I married his mother in 1980, when he was a little over two years old, was basically sound. But perhaps as with all teenage boys and their dads, step or no, by the time he was thirteen we were somewhat, though never disastrously, at odds. As a writer of poems rather than a swinger of baseball bats, a caster of fly fishing rods, a shooter of pheasant rifles, and as someone who had sat at the feet of various saintly shuyukh, or Sufi Masters, in particular the great scholar and Qutub Shaykh Muhammad ibn al Habib of Fez, buried now in his Zawiyya in Meknes, I thought I might try to instill some wisdom into the proceedings as the seal of our spiritual bond.

This book has been in manuscript since I wrote it in 1991, a year after our large cross-country move from California to Philadelphia, from the sunny beaches and horrendously high-priced accommodations of Santa Barbara, to the four-season'd urban life of Philadelphia, original home of my wife and Farid's mother, Malika. There was some excitement in all this, and mountains of adjustment for a thirteen year-old boy having left friends behind and working his way into new circles of peers in a very new and often suspicious environment. So I was also conscious of extending a hand of understanding, both in real terms and in these poems for him, and hopefully for others in similar situations (though I eschew poetry as sociology, which it has often become in our present day). The fact that his father (renowned British photographer, Peter Sanders) resided in London with a new family (his three half-sisters, and his full brother, Mukhtar, two years his senior), while he lived in Philadelphia with us and his American half-sister, Salihah, who was nine at the time, was the actual and emotional environment of his early teenagehood. Caught between biological father and stepfather and two families, one far off in England and his immediate family in America, was certainly for him a thickening of his familial plot. This was also the maze I made my way through in this series of poems, veering off here and there into my own brand of "magical realism," then coming back to facts and "things as they are," or at least attempting to.

Connecting with people, especially in our immediate families, is a dimension of high-voltage dynamics that have perplexed folk through the ages. Shakespeare would be nothing if all the stretched and stretching lines of relationship were easy. From Genesis on, the actions of siblings and honoring of parental connections and the ever-shifting menus on the part of parents themselves of what to impart, what to hold back, what to expect, what to let go of, are multifarious. Diving into this domain, then, was as much an impulse of my poetic imagination as a personally domestic one.

But after emerging from his teen years, shining in college and moving upward in his career, a trustworthy, sane and spiritual person of great integrity, Farid will be thirty-one in August of 2008. And I'm taking this opportunity to dust off the manuscript and publish these poems today in honor of his wedding in his new home of Zurich, Switzerland, to Swiss native, Tina Theler, who seems in our eyes and obviously in his, to be a perfect mate. I intend this little book to be a blessing for their life together… a raised toast (with the wine of God's wisdom), and an affirmation.

After all its meanderings, homilies, historical memories, surreal asides and linguistic bridges, I think the core reverberant line is *"You've been grafted to my root,"* which turned out to be the central discovery for me early in the writing of these poems, and which sealed the deal for us both, and continues to do so to this day, and to the end of our days, with God's Grace and Permission.

O God, drown me in the essence of the Ocean of
Divine Solitude, so that I neither see nor hear nor find
nor feel except through It.
ʿABD AS-SALAM IBN MASHISH

The drop became a fountain, and the fountain grew into
   a river,
Which river became reunited to the ocean of eternity.
SHEIKH ABULFAIZ FAIYAZI

All Your waves and breakers have rolled over me
PSALM 42. 7

Launch out in the deep.
SAINT LUKE V

## 1  WHITE EAGLE IN A PIT

There's a lot to be said for
growing up. I don't remember noticing it much
until pubic hair. Then the body

takes off in all
directions. Big feet. Boniness. Boners. Brainstorms.
It must feel strange, inflating that way into
space. Touching other

worlds by increased dimension alone. Trying on
thoughts never before entertained, voices imitated
nothing like your own. Skewed
attitudes, screwed-on faces,
one of which might be yours.

The reluctant largesse of being
about to be fourteen,
strapped to the
seasonal wheel that pushes the
past behind it as it
rotates forward. Ironing you out.
Making you more dimensional. Taller.

Perpetual summer with collapsing panels in it of
winters and deep dark troughs. Where you may find
oil rolling into braids with water. Gut
messages. Lengths of time
lengthening. And there it is! *White*

*eagle in a pit!* It

rises all of a sudden –

*Catch it!*

6/11

## 2  FIRST DAYS

It's funny, but since you're not my
biological son, I never had the
experience of your first days the way you and
I had the experience of your sister's first days, in
Granada, when we walked
hand in hand to *El Hospital de los Pobres* to see her
the morning after she was
born, and you were
four years old.

It was a
short walk down the cobblestone alleys of the
gypsy quarter where we lived, out through the
Moorish gate, around the
Fascist fountain and a few blocks
further into the Catholic echo-chamber of
birth, agony and death, Spanish-style, full of
zigzag wounds and the resonance of blood.

Your
mother was desperate: Garlic-breath'd gypsies
had filled her room at the
crack of dawn with themselves and
everything but goats.
The starched,
black-eyebrowed nurses hadn't

brought her any water since the birth
("*the kitchen isn't
open yet*"), and your
sister hadn't been
given the breast but a few
drops of chamomile tea instead, in
spite of my instructions a few hours earlier
in perfect Spanish
(odd custom I'm convinced leads to their
incessant chain smoking, denied
those first tastes of deep reality in
breast-milk, as I
now pointed out to all the doctors heftily
puffing away on strong Gaulois-type cigarettes).

We
rescued your mother and sister from this hell, you
taking on your
most serious air,
helped your mother out of bed a scant
five hours after the birth, wrapped your tiny round-faced
sister in a flannel blanket, your
mother limping out between us, we
supporting her on either side, the

Holy Family
escaping Pharaoh's army out the
high arches of the

hospital entrance, through a threatening
throng of gypsy women reputed to
steal new babies right out of their
mothers' arms, and

filled with determination, you consoling, solicitous and
calm, we splurged and hailed a
rattletrap yellow & black checkerboard taxi
home.

                6/11

## 3   AS FOR US

As for us, something about your
two-year old enthusiasm, running to me on
short legs, arms out, head nimbus of
blond curls, as I was
courting your mother. I would

pick you up and lift you high.
You sat between us when we
got married, as if you were
giving your mother away to me, and even
came with us on the
wedding night, so that
instead of shunting you off for the
big event of our marriage
an immediate connection with a new dad would be made –

we took you with us to the
little apartment I'd rented and gave you a
big piece of apple pie & ice-cream and a brand new
Tinker Toy set so you'd be well-fed and
fully occupied as your mom and I looked
moon-eyed at each other until you
safely conked out, and the
night could open up its
starry blankets for us.

We all three spent our honeymoon days at the San Antonio Zoo,
your mom and I lying on the grass together in a

green mist of psychic cloud, you
running around in front of the
cages, yelling out each
new discovery.

Your genetic connection to me was how
deeply I had you in my heart.

In England a year later, that one day of
light snow, you and I built a
snowman together in the back yard of our house
and then bombed it to smithereens with
anti-idolatry snowballs. You've often said it's your
first memory of all, those
fuzzy snapshots in motion we have
lodged in our tabernacular domes.

You've been
grafted to my root.

I watch you
sprout.

6/11

4   ASTRONOMICAL REFLECTOR

A boy is
smelly socks and embarrassing underwear,
collections in closets, baseball cards, odd rocks, old
magazines, opinions adhered to with a
bless&eacute;d fanaticism even in the face of
error.

Plans, usually monetary, the
purchase of more technology, never enough
time to just do nothing, with its
bureaucrat bedfellow: *Boredom*. Then there are
crisscross rafters, gargantuan bicycles, glory playing
bugles, disappointment the size of Macy's,
rivalry in everything the size of the
Roman Colosseum,

the continuous obligation to be clothed, flim-flams,
secrets, secrets with royal seals, secrets with
body-fluids, genuine secrets from other
dimensions, a comradeship with
heroes and society's discards,
an almost uncritical acceptance of media superstars as well as
*bona fide* champions,

a nonchalance about the Big Questions, a
younger child's uncanny perspicacity in such
matters, a vulnerable blond and warm-blooded
streak connecting you with
infancy, your own infancy

shading you from behind
like a giant astronomical reflector on a
mountaintop from a
sun whose fiery explosions will

broil us all anyway
in the end.

　　　　　　　　　　　　　　6/12

## 5   I WANT TO TALK TO YOU

O.K. I want to talk to you in a way my own father
never talked to me. I can't remember
a single conversation we ever had. We
never talked about anything important. *Can you
believe it!* It's like
explorers taking off their clothes and running
stark naked into uncharted
territory with
no ammunition, no amulets, no articles of
trade – you've got to
make it all up from scratch when your own
male dad can't transmit anything of weight to you to
use! But all he had to do (not even

gray woolen monk's robes, astrolabes or arcane
scrolls) was just share a bit of
candor and reality, a few
simple exchanges on a park-bench, a nod of
understanding that meant something more than just
a male conspiracy against mom's
enveloping dimension.

Not that I've got that much to transmit to you
from masculine expertise, neither
boat-building skills nor computer wizardry, all the way
down to a suave and cavalier ability to make a
living without expending
desperate energy, I haven't even got street-smarts
hustler mentality!

But still I can
hope to give you

some candor and reality, or at least try to make it
possible to find
some of it
together. A bit of

candor and reality.

                                                                    6/12

## 6   HOLES

Some people walk along in the world for years and
never fall down any of its holes. They may not even
think they walk a thin crust, at the very lip.

Others are in a hole from birth. Superhuman
strength or inexplicable Grace gives them
the ghetto-green
leather wings they need to lift free,
or else they
paper its curved walls with lifetimes of sad tales and their
inevitable consequences. Endless loops of
inevitable consequences, like
lingering clouds of gunpowder
in empty doorways.

Everyone's destiny
sits very still under a strange hat in the shape of a
walking foot on a glass table in front of a
round mirror – *a complete
mystery!* Some are given

everything and
still have nothing. Some are given nothing but a
giant black boat made of cardboard boxes that
sits in the street like Noah's ark but won't admit of
pairs of anything. When the flood comes,
scraps of sodden cardboard
float downstream.

Others see what they're given, and the fine glass
tubing that connects
the gift with the Giver, even when the
Giver is camouflaged behind trees of cloud and clouds of
weightless trees.

Our destinies have such unforeseeable wobbles in them, dips
up or down. They could
land us in the Emerald City of supreme meaningfulness,
each moment outlined in excitable silver, or
dump us down one of those holes in the earth that are actually
breathing vents through deep darkness, actually
wriggling tunnels the exact sizes of our

bodies that
open out onto the Infinite
anyway.

6/16

7   SAGE ADVICE

The father in overalls of plywood and shoes of
Galapagos tortoise shells tried to give some
sage advice to his son, so he put his
face out of a clock face and slowly rotated his
hands. He sat outside the

front door and every time his son left the house he
winked or shrugged or bashfully bounced a
baseball bat against his shoe.

The father wore two rosebushes for a tie, crossed and
knotted properly at top. The thorns did their
work through his shirt until
droplets of blood formed a mosaic of red
dots against white, but he
refused to stretch his arms straight out to each side.

He did try
shotguns across his knee in country tweeds,
computer printout pinstripes tailored to fit snug,
iron tennis rackets, grappling hooks and outdated
mountaineering gear. Finally
exhausted with the roles of father he felt
inadequate to play, putting two freshly-shot

rabbits onto the floor, their fur matted
brown, their eyes stiff, he gazed forward into
his son's face, gazed and gazed until

both faces saw one image for a moment before

breaking into

separate redwood trees.

6/23

## 8  ANCESTRAL FATHERS

Funny how after beginning to write these
poems to you without your

knowing it, a new quality has entered into our
life between us. As if somehow we were

both made more transparent, me become more paternally
porous thinking about you, you

picking up on my
inner attention to you –

existing more in
each other's world.

Do I want to write a Swiss Family Robinson tree house you can
walk into and climb up ingeniously fashioned

spiral stairways to a wondrous
vista? That image of

looking out over somewhere from a
lofty height, "Cortez" and his

men amazed in Darien, father and son on a
high cliff with proper

N.C. Wyeth sunset over a distant seascape? And words.
Strong as the flap of ascending gulls' wings, softly

exchanged, from stomach-deeps, yet so
simple you could use them as

floor plans to build an
entire city from. Levels and plumbs. Saw-screech

echoing from nearby valleys. Hammering
foundations from only

a few words exchanged between
father and son standing in any old weeds

on any old cliff overlooking anywhere. Double-images of
ancestral fathers like

jittery outlines in photographic sepia
come down around us for some

eerie overtones...

                                            6/24

9   SEX

Sex is a symphony to the poor –
it lifts to heights so
unlike usual day. Deft intimations
of celestial weightlessness. Vertical smooth and
rounded sensations
more like music.

Sex is a car-handle – *hey! It can be
too hot to handle!* It can open on
naugahyde seat covers and be like the
slopping of ice cream. Sex is when imperfect human bodies
become perfect shimmering black velvet temples of
spontaneous delight, deep sonics and a
hook into
genetic rivers flowing

forward and backward at the
same rate. There's actually no
trifling with it, as much as it
seems like a toy for us to
bounce around. It reaches
to our roots. Roots us to the
ground. Can
avalanche with giant
boulders to our deaths, or
gently crest, lavish grace of aching sweetness,
agonies of separation splashingly

joined for a moment in hushed
deliverance like a
slow cortege of birch-bark canoes approaching
mist-veiled estuaries of
totemic significance, staring giant
animal-faces looming out of the fog
at our sides.

Alchemists, in their diagrams of
pure gold resulting from the
joining of opposites, and mystics
singing of their
annihilation in God's powerful embrace
have always used the metaphor of sexual union
to represent the ecstasy and
mystery of their

joy.

*Find out why.*

6/24

## 10   THAT SOUND

Oh my dear son, not of my
flesh, but of my
bone, we are all waiting for the
pure sound, as if
out on a point of land at sea under a
full moon, wanting to
hear the song, a voice, straining to
hear that sound, each one of us
clear, as if
first of all men to
hear and
respond to its call. It's a
whipping wind, a wild
promontory, jagged
clouds across a
black scrim. Then the

lights go up and we find we're in a
whitewashed room with an old man
next to an old
woman sitting with
glistening nets all around them, and even they aren't
more than a faint murmur of that sound. They

may have heard it, and they may
not have heard it. It's for
each one of us

to respond.

6/24

## 11  THAT FIRST MEMORY

We looked out our mid-winter window in Norwich, England,
onto a
backyard being dusted with snow. There's *never* any
snow in Norwich! But the snow kept
falling. Finally we
ran out in it, you
three years old, shouting
"*Let's make a snowman!*" Not much to
make one with, snow so soft and
powdery, but we

scraped one together, and pretty soon not a bad
snow-dude appeared, mostly a
tall mound, hardly any head, hardly any
arms at all, but I put my
knitted sock-cap on it to give it
class. Your mother leaned
out the window and threw us a
carrot for nose, and we looked around for
stones for eyes, no

coal nuggets near, until finally we had a
real old-fashioned *bona fide*
snowman worth crowing about. We
crowed. Your mom
crowed from the kitchen. The snowman was well-
crowed. Suddenly I had a flash about sculpted images,
idols, molded to cast

shadows, monotheism's
constant contention against them, prophet Abraham's
victory for
imageless Majesty, and said, "*Hey, this is an
idol, we have to
knock it down – only God is real!* " You

loved this idea, and clapped your
mitts together, yelling, "*Yeah, let's
destroy the idol!*" Your mom disagreeing and
"*Oh-no*"ing disappointedly from the
window. We scooped up snowballs and started
pelting the snowman to
slush, slowly
eroding his head, bombarding his
torso to
a pile of shapeless snow again, really getting our
backs into it, "*Take this, you idol, and this* (splat!), *and
this!* " Laughing

until we were exhausted and
done. And you've remained
deeply impressed by this moment, saying it's your
very first memory, that stubborn

powerful fiction that actually
shapes our consciousnesses
all the rest of our days.

11/6

## 12 AT THE HEART OF THE ATOM

What would you expect at the
center of the universe, behind
veils of matter, at the
heart of the atom?

You'd probably say
a baseball game, eternally sublime, everyone in
cloud-white and sky-blue uniforms, bats of
lightning-bolts, balls of
radiant suns. A billion innings without
a moment of boredom, everyone at peak, happily
playing ball. Infinite *thwap* of fist into mitt, infinite
crack of bat.

Or serenely going on at the center of the universe,
a Japanese Nôh drama, dry tap of
drum, clack of woodblocks, low strike of
gong, foot-shuffle, cloth-swish, intense masked figures
speaking in tight clouds of sound that
slowly disperse. Fan snaps open.
Worlds appear. Fan snaps shut. A figure
larger than life half-turns with a face of smooth moon.

Or else, at the center of the atom
ratchety
chaos of Hindu-like gyrations,
arm-flings gracefully
extending raw mountain ranges,

eyes swiveling
vividly in black-tinted sockets as
shouts as volcanic as earth's first moments
echo through space with
flashing red fireworks.

Or else, at the Supreme Center, slow-motion
silence of plants urging
upward and opening, that
hushed mechanism of no-time in which time
appears
caught by surprise in a
green doorway, naked.
A room of energized coolness, open window with
blousy gauze curtains, odors of
jasmine so languorous as to be
visible, strands of
sand-colored nothingness knotting and unknotting in the
air.

Or at the very Center of the center,
absolute heart of All,
tunnel within tunnel, depth within depth,
drop through the bottom, dive
through the bottom of a
sea of darkness so deep no
motion is possible, no breath
drawn, but still it's
perfectly serene. Where the

Voice of God, spaceless, writes
silences in water, emptiness in a
ripple, phrases of
articulate light
everywhere.

                                          6/26

## 13   ACTUAL BASEBALL

As for actual baseball, it's just
not my game. I know you
wish it were
otherwise. I wish there were

two of me, one to fulfill your
expectations of a dad, the other to show you the
integrity of a man being who he is and
pretty much

will be, with
occasional ecstatic
excursions out of the norm. I've
taken you to a few games, shown

interest in the players, gotten
out there to throw the
ball around a few times, and I
love to see you happy. But I'll

admit I'm not very convincing.
It's equally
hard for you to get excited about poetry, your
Walt Whitman report notwithstanding.

There must be cosmic justice at work here.
Me up to bat with catchy phrases and a few
verbal homeruns, you at a
blank page with pen in hand, and, after a

few thought-balls, high and wide, the words
bob first to
first, then second, third if luck's
with you, with an occasional

home base slide of punctuation and
fully expressed ideas in a
sea of crowd-noise and
dictionarial verbiage.

## 14 SUPERNATURAL SON

Ah, since you're not my
natural son, you can be my
*supernatural* son! No actual genes of mine

swim in your blood, your flesh doesn't
resemble mine, though since I've been your
dad from the time you were two, we now have a definite

family resemblance, leaping over
genetic fact like some sleek green grasshopper of
supernatural light.

Your life and mine came together out of
as many possibilities as there are
gnats in summer over still waters.

I've popped you into my shoulder-bag,
stuffed you in there
with my notebook and pen,

worn down good shoe leather climbing around
with you in there,
my dear supernatural son.

## 15  LIMITS

The limits to this life are like
the unlikelihood of finding ants building

perfectly geometrical pyramids out of
crumbs on your morning toast, haloed by a

stray sunbeam. Men walked the earth with
their eyes in the clouds, dreamt of

bird's wings out of
Leonardo Da Vincian contraptions until

the Wright Brothers made an airplane of
wood struts and canvas and took

off into the skies. Atoms invisible to the
eye had a full life out of view, spent

millennia in secret until electron-microscopes
found them naked in their lairs. Now we can even

manipulate them to do tricks for us, but
only to certain limits. The creation as

created sits in an established kingdom with
archways of spun diamond and fields of

emerald grass under a sun of
intense observation already

singing in its limits, even stretching the song at times
to near inscrutability. But God's

Throne is not unoccupied, and the
margins to existence are real. It's just

our task as realists to stretch our own personal
limits to meet those

already cosmically set. For there may be
worlds big enough to herd bison giant as

canyons through before our
lips meet the lips of the

limits of this life in a
kiss in which our

eyes also meet to exchange
the sweetest embrace since

bees first pollinated
blazing hibiscus flowers in the

earth's pale coral dawn.

6/30

## 16 WOMAN

You were
born of woman, brought
up by woman, and she shall
be by your side somehow in the
elusive chemical elements that
spin in something as
small as a dewdrop or as
unending as the sky. Some posit the

Eternal Feminine as the endless summation and basis of
life, her tragic
stamina and renewal. The
Prophet said
"*Paradise lies at the feet of mothers.*"
Her eyes like house-windows casting down
glances scanning the street until her
child returns,
her ears like a forest late at night listening to the
padding of very small feet across
very thin needles and dry leaves.

She loves
a slowly accumulating warm recognition of her being, and
that you
listen to her as an equal, and give her
noble entrance into the named and numerous
items of your world.

Her voice stays with us, the melodious
feminine we
already heard through the
walls of the womb. It didn't need

ferns and tall grasses for the
graceful heron of her voice to
stalk through, it was already

music in flight, music in
massaging hands, our whole bodies
cradled in her sound.

                                                               6/30-7/1

## 17  MORE SAGE ADVICE

The father tried to tell his son something about
women and wooden gates
closed on his knees, and he got that
sorrowful look under moose-antlers that linked him up with
grandfathers from the "old country," as well as
bronze aborigines sitting on a rock at cave-front, deep inner walls
recently painted with magically powerful
pregnant kangaroos in
x-ray.

*"Nothing like a little bit of knowledge to fool you,"* but with
women you can never have enough. Elusive forever, the
best you can do is suspend the contest and let her
skillfully folded paper boats skim across the surface of your water
as you look up through its ripples
from the muddy bottom
at a sunlight that always seems new.

*"Now, don't think you can take them for granted, but
don't let them plant you head-first in their
back gardens either."* He piled up
tomes on Queen Elizabeth the First and Catherine the
Great, bountiful boat of Russia, who had
slits in her dress for the gentlemen of the court,
though that might have been just a dour and disapproving
male historian mongering scarlet lies to disenfranchise her.
Men can be grim. Masters at disapproval. Torn by attraction
one minute to sky, next minute to
earth.

The father sat back on pillows of recent shipwreck and
stared at the wall with his son beside him
and told of his healing intimacy with his mother,
her strengths and consistencies, and how, at the
topmost Mongolian tundra in the dead of winter, with the
sky tilted down dark slate-gray turquoise,
in thick woolen embroidered garments, the woman, noble as stone,
builds a fire under a cauldron and only
briefly looks at her soft round face in the water before
stirring the coals, her sheep stoically
waiting outside, black eyes
under shy eyelashes.

Which is why
he had so much trouble explaining to his
son who woman is

(seeing in her beauty
such patience and serenity),

since
they both were
men.

7/1

## 18  LEGACY

I

I wonder if a father looked deeply inside himself he'd find
what he really wanted for his son, or whether he'd find
as much bewilderment in the world for his son as he
finds for himself, surrounded by the
roaring iron lions of commerce, the
vivid dream-figures of
Quest, with all its cardiac pressures and
sudden, occasional divine clarities, but
the world like a domain of green prairie as far as
the naked eye can see from
one curved sky to another, and the
clouds in the son's life as
unreadable in their puffing masses as they are to
his father, now, on earth, among now's mortal crowd.

Would the high-wire aerialist envision his
son in white tights on a silver bicycle in
crossing spotlights at the same
hair-line between
daring and death, feeling
the same mastery, precision, thrill of
one more death-defying danger foiled?

The drum rolls.
The spotlight comes to rest.
A hush. The father is gray, his once firm muscles slack.

Throws off his cape and
out of his chest steps a son who stands on the
thin wire above the crowd perfectly poised, and

out of his chest steps his son with a sweeping bow, and

out of *his* chest steps his son who leaps in the air

and lands on the
wire on one hand.


2

"*Ah, I leave you such an imperfect world,*" says the
father who's missed the point.
Standing in the midst of it all but thinking he's
somehow the author of it, and that somehow he's unable to stop the
destructive drift of it.

A king in his throne room playing with
wind-up toys on his
ivory table for his son, while
just behind him is the
avalanche of One Eyed Dragon Mountain, and the
son in brocade has to
walk without royal robes through the
falling streams of that avalanche, seeing if he can

charm the rocky chunks to slow-motion,
charm the down-drag of gravity to
soften its pull and bring
this life into peaceful quiescence at last.

*Every man's task.*


3

The world as I found it,
brown nut in a loose bag,

reindeer on the tundra,
bright skies, wise skies,

knock your pipe on the washstand,
little door in a big house,

smooth rope hanging in a well,
bluejay on a clothesline,

desktop cluttered with books,
alchemist's knucklebones,

flash out the window, start the car,
staircase in a clockwise spiral,

mouse-noses twitching over breakfast,
enter the world a noisy guest,

leave the world a sober one,
while you're here sweep the floor,

while you're here listen to birdsong,
the world as I found it,

leave it alone,
wear it out

next to your skin,
the world as I found it,

brown nut in a loose bag,
the world as I found it,

my son and all sons after him.

7/2 – 7/4

## 19  THE YOU IN ALL THIS

I

But the you in all this,
who wants to fly off in your own glueless airplane,
a bullet circling above domesticated space,

who wants to wear your hair
so no childish blond curl show,
cut close with razor-etched emblem in back,

who wants to wear cool clothes, personally
chosen, socially judged,

who wants to face the shifting fiery grids of the
world on your own, your
own home-grown wings fluttering and
folding about you, faintly bat-wing, adolescently
angelic. *Yeah... Tentative.*

Emotional yo-yo. Up like the wooden sideshow pellet
struck by a giant hammer to show your strength
ringing the bell with a

jubilant "clang," or
agonizingly sliding to the bottom as if
sinking in quicksand, *Oh God!*

2

What do I know of your future, with your
face of a skyscraper in Twenty-First Century architecture,
eyes looking out 100 story windows onto the
whole town you own, Park Place, Marvin Gardens, hotels and all,
stadiums where your teams in
silver Adidas play, your malls like
tropical vegetation along tunneling stems, Art Deco smooth, painted
pastel colors from every
sunrise on earth,

your hands filled with the bounty of He Whose
Invisibility doesn't diminish His
gentle power over the spin of each insect
giddily crossing space, your own rise or fall, our
facing forward together in the end,
in the same direction, toward Death's bright tunnel,
one generation only
one step ahead of the next.

The father provides the echo – the
son's voice moves up into it and
inhabits it, making it
his own.

My only advice is:
*do not adhere to the way of those who*
*deny God's splendor*
*that lights everything with His*

*Smile.*
*Their projects do not endure.*

See for yourself. Make a few
slow eye-sweeps across
time, a few gradual
glances across the
globe. High towers
fall. Tyrants get
marched to the
wall.


3

Son, if I could go up through your bloodstream and
look out through your eyes for a
moment, nothing would be gained. The same
world with
different eyelashes would
face us both. Your

gestures, all your own, feet inching forward on
golden tiles, your
alert ears at their
peak hearing
peacock's scream across the
dark river's rush, and your own
breath-pulse driving the
liveliness that's

yours. Intake and
hold, then
outbreath through abandoned
houses of mortar and thought, flimsy as the
night-motels of
hungry spiders spun taut between
boughs. And your

particular glances, facial expressions at
signals whose ciphers can
only be deciphered by the
submarine movements of your own heart, spreading out
invisible decoder charts on your
own heart's table, phantom maps drawn on
transparent deer-hide, mysterious places of
no remarkable quality, where so much
beginning takes place unbeknownst even to
you.

7/10

## 20  READINESS FOR DEATH

We can only write so many poems, throw
so many baseballs, solve so many
insoluble problems, imagine
so many universes, play
so many computer games before we
leave them all the way a mist lifts up from
fields at dawn and evaporates entirely away.

Then we will be looking at the Next World through
smokeless glasses, we'll be
watching the total eclipse of ourselves directly without
burning our corneas. There will be
flakes as large as lakes containing
intricately carved rose-quartz palaces of thought
floating in a slanted light-ray of indigo
purple
pulsing a puddle of audible
glory around us when we die.

It opens like a loving vulva to let us in, and then
all our works lie in a tiny heap on a
mummified table back in
earth's clear sunlight as if back down a
long hall just past a
beaded curtain, someone playing a
drunken tune on an out-of-tune piano
behind a paper-thin wall. But we'll be
dead. Our complete works fit

between two black covers
which can be
opened or closed. We would wish to have
written them otherwise, more
flights, stranger angles, more
wisdom, but they are
just as they are,
surrounded by the
space-moat of our deaths,
beaming radio isotopes in the
direction of our afterlives
as well as the
direction of the life that continues among the blithe ones
left living on earth.

I always try to travel light, death stopping its
vehicle right by us at any moment, the shivering
skeleton of a surprise bus that opens its
skinny door to let us in.

I try to be aware of
what's in my pockets, what
words have been written last in my
poem notebooks, what thoughts are coiling in my
head, what
gelatinous or teleportable
motions sudsing in my heart, the last way I've left

my loved ones, what
remains disarrayed in my room as

evidence for or against me, because
as we step off one moment onto the
slippery disc of the next it might
suddenly take off with us and

that's it.

7/12

## 21  THE TROUBLE IS

The trouble is, I've become, in my own
eyes at least, a lot like my
own father, his general
shape and look (me bearded these last
thirty years, he never) but
his thickness around the
middle (he was
flat-bottomed, I've got two
basketballs for a butt so I'm
told), a small
pot belly like his, and just as
he was I was
skinny until eight
years ago, he also, slim and dark when young, and then

ballooned, maybe we were
very much alike then as now, me fifty,
many of the
same looks, it's almost
discouraging, growing up not
liking the
look of his body,
feeling almost
embarrassed for him, he
no model of masculinity, slope-shouldered,
rubber-tire hipped, but smiling and
full of natural charm, witty, even later when
stroke-befuddled –
gracious even though befogged.

I want to
accept him in his
lifelong confusion, his
reticence, the way he
stepped back from an
embrace. I want to
let him be, totally
human, bound to his
own private destiny as a
man. I see him

in his own size before I was
even born, waltzing across a
polished floor with my
mother. Old photograph. But in my
memory he was
ineffectual, our
generation's shame, our fathers seemed so
wrongheaded and
ineffectual. He

tied himself tightly to the mast of
middle-class respectability
passing by those
mesmerizing island-bound sirens whose
weird wails could drive you
mad, or put you in
touch with wild
cosmos, their
aching close harmonies like the
baying of timber wolves. Stuffing wax globs of

society's unexamined opinions in his
ears to pass by unscathed, my (in my eyes at least)
underdeveloped dad.

But I
*wanted* to be scathed, deeply scarred by
the extremes of this life, see the sirens'
rolling yellow cats' eyes up close, run my
fingers through their
snaky hair, something my

father would never dare, nor dare to
hear them with
naked ear. The man was

only partially alive, we
all are, who

live in fear.

7/13

## 22  HAPPINESS

"Come right in, my son, through this
scalloped arch into the darkened
octangular room bathed in
blue light – let's sit at this
table and see what's
what. Where you might go. What you might

see. For example, take that small
cedar wood box down from the shelf. Open it.
Don't be afraid. Slow green steam out the sides of the
lid? Well, maybe.
*Go on, open it.* Now you're in

a tropical paradise, purplish shores slanted into
silverish waters, dolphin-rings
surrounding it. You stowed away and
were the first to arrive, swimming
to shore. A
dark-skinned shimmering
woman approaches, offering
coconut
filled with nectar, fiery
hibiscus in her hair.

O.K. Now we're back in the room.
Take that seal tusk, the one by your elbow etched with
feathery black shape of whale-creature. You
got it in your hand? Now you're
facing sheer ice-cliffs looming straight up to

infinity like an endless shrill
steam-whistle, you've got your
ice-hooks, your team, your men and dogs, and a
vision of God in your head no hardship can
shake, but you want to
taste its reality as poignantly in your flesh as if
your taste buds could tell. Wind
rips your clothes, the tent blows away, a
comforting blizzard covers you.
Big light comes down.

O.K. Back in the
room again, bathed in blue.
Maps by your
leg there. Unroll them. *They're
blank?* Put your
thumb in one place, and your
forefinger wherever, draw a

circle that suddenly bursts into
flame with a
perfectly harmonious
transparent globe in the center in which
trees and brook breathe the same air, lynx and
cougar lithely prowl, whole
canyons are backdrop to the
soaring of fledgling falcons, and you are
standing here by yourself, you've walked for five
days, the last day on
short rations, this is
nothing like sitting in a room with

video games, there are
real insects down your shirt here, sticky
burrs inside your
socks, sweat
blackening your
hat-brim. This is as

far away from any kind of happiness as you could have
imagined, and yet
you're happy. Air-currents seem to
jump-start from your
heartbeats. You've stopped being
edgy at your own shadow. All
paranoia swept away on an
updraft. You stand in

total wonder, two boots sunk in
creek-mud, each
leaf-twitch in breeze felt by
twinge of
cheek
covered with hair. You're
hooked-up now pal, empty as
sky and just as
wide.

Silent pure
soul at the

center of it."

7/17

## 23 LIKE WHEN YOU WAVE AT A TRAIN AND THE TRAIN HOOTS BACK AT YOU

I

The universe of our actual, measurable
lives in it, I mean our
*actual* shapes, our *actual*
shades of color, length of arm, color of eye,
ways of striding, talking, the

*I don't know*, unpresumable
miracle of it, in its
little things, passing along a thimble to someone sewing
that becomes a
volcano erupting in the
Philippines, *no*, I mean something
very simple really, the
getting up and crossing a room, going

back to the
momentary point of origin, not even
thinking of the epic plotting of points ever-shifting and
stuttering into new
relationships in a single lifetime, as many
points as unknown stars, behind the ones we see, the ones
we can't see –

responsive, reflecting, reflexive
world of us we live in, that
lives in us with double intensity,

like when you
wave at a train and the
train hoots back at you, effecting and effected.

Whistle the birdsong you
just heard in the forest and it
sings it back to you.

Ask someone at night, your own self
giving you up for
lost in the maze of a
new, unfamiliar
neighborhood, and
that person just happens to be
going to the same place, and you can
happily follow her.

Like cutting away the universe in dreamtime and finding
dream creatures cutting away from their own side as well, with a
near inevitable
tunnel breakthrough as in the
Chunnel under the English Channel between
France and England.

I've read and reread what I've been
writing in these poems to find out what's left
out, what
makes the whole of it
unsatisfying somehow, wondering if they're
honest enough, candid and real enough after all,
or have I not gotten to you, in your

own reality, which I can only
know in partial coded messages, the limited knowledge

all of us have with each other, with a
greater or lesser degree of interpretive accuracy.
Do the poems need more
concrete narrative thread, more
personal details? But more than just your
life's being
embraced here –

More confession of how I love you, and
hope I've held you in
high enough esteem, and given you at least
heart-nourishment as armor for the
more or less pitiless
voyage into…


2

Voyage into heaven by way of the
sharp dark rocks of earth, the
entangling consumer temples, the
now more or less universalized secular goal of mankind
for better and greater numbers of
*Things*

for which I have no hunger at all, and

worry about the excessiveness of yours.
I actually fell asleep at the end of that
stanza, trailing off at *"voyage into..."*, a phenomenon that
takes place from time to time, and really
surprises me, since I'm
writing along, albeit late at night, with full
intensity, moving pen into elusive territories, then I
fall asleep right in the
middle of a
tasty little passage, trick of
middle age, no doubt –

But now I know what was
missing: *The basketball backboard!*

You saved up your money and bought it in July, middle of
our first muggy Philadelphia summer, regulation
iron pole and backboard, free-standing, regulation
height, needing to be
sunk deep in the ground with cement.
I fished out the instructions from the heavy rectangular box
and found it needed
900 lbs of dry weight cement to be
properly installed. *Nine Hundred
Pounds!* I

staggered at the
thought. Months went
by. *"Let's wait for
cooler weather. We can't go out in this."* The
thought of it hung like Coleridge's albatross across

my shoulders. Weekend after
weekend, help from other men being
blissfully
elusive as well. One weekend I actually
drove to the
Home Improvement Center by myself and
just looked at 900 lbs of cement, and
staggered again! *Twenty-three bags*! Put it off a
few more weekends. Its image
smoked and fumed all through the
writing of these
poems, a guilt of not
doing this for you, until finally last
weekend I decided to
tackle it no matter what –
went back to the Home Improvement, this time took you with me.

An old man who looked like he was partly composed of
cement dust walked by with his grown son, I
stopped him and asked him what he thought, he agreed,
looking at the instruction sheet, in
slow Philly black man's drawl I was so
happy to hear, "*Yeah,
900 lbs sure do seem like a lot of
cement to me!*" So ended up buying only
eight bags, 320 lbs, brought them home,
covered them with
blue plastic tarp against the rain
(it's now all the way into
November), and then

last weekend we did it!
Dug the hole, post-hole digger and
digging rod and shovel, mixed the
cement in blue plastic washtub,
you shivering a little in the
wintry chill of that
Sunday afternoon, poured the
first tub of cement in, then the second, third,
mixing and sweating and getting arm-sore and
joking, you practicing your first year
Spanish on me while we
worked, me finally saying in
exasperated Spanish, "*Que me manden un ayudante mejor
que un mosquito el tiempo siguiente!*" since you'd
wimped out on me a few times. And while we
worked, your mother came out with a tray of
soup and saltines and said what had
just crossed my mind a few
scant minutes before: "*This
reminds me of your
snowman in Norwich!*" And the
connection was made!


3

You wave at a passing train, and the
engineer might feel

nonchalant enough to hoot his
horn at you, one blast or

two, as he
travels down the track.

You stand in the
street amid the

desperately homeless, and
a net of spidery

lights might fall on you, one hand with
coins outstretched, one foot on the

way to
give comfort (Whitman in the

Civil War soldiers' tents, administering to
amputees, writing last

letters for them, kissing matted
beards in death).

A dripping faucet in this room wants to divert me from my
task, our black

cat is in an
exploratory mood, and I want to

raise all the
weight of these words to a great

unifying chorus bringing
migrating birds over

train-tracks together with
the blank future rolling toward us like

stampeding bison, the identical ones that
vanished from the prairies in the

past, come
round again, past and

future looped together, and assure you, by God, that
all is well, all's in

place and
accounted for, perfect –

We turn like chameleons
yellow or blue with the

prevailing backdrop, and I often
wonder at the

puzzle-pieces in you that
no one but

you and Allah can
know – why you turn

yellow at one thing, blue at
another, psychological

streams coming together in a clenched
waterspout, burgeoning

clouds of good fortune and rain, recent
mercy from above, down

upon us.
Your

season of salutations is
near. Be

innocent forever.
Nothing is gained by cynicism but a

sneer.
Rainbows have bled back into their

beams.
*Angels to thy rest.*


4

But in this actual world we're born in
it's as if there were nothing
normal in loving God, or in
seeing the

world of form as if it were frail
latticework onto the Infinite, with
wide spaces in the mesh revealing
gold meadows for every shadowy disaster, wide
skies for every claustrophobic tragedy.

In this life it's as if
it were abnormal to go
with light heart through the world like a
traveler on an expense account even though
penniless, ordering the best vintage
water from tumbling country streams, the finest
delicacy from a tray of stray sunbeams.

Or, if this is too picturesque (which it is, almost
maudlin, though the
tone is right), if it's just a matter of seeing
the actors and events of the moments of our lives as if behind their
scrawny, pompous, dissembling, mask-like
faces with wiggling eyebrows and mouths like the
evening news,
the faceless void of light and harmonious singing were
winking straight at us with an expression
falling somewhere between
mischief and majesty.

The world has been given to us with all its flags of
opposition unfurled.

Certain sealed scrolls wait to be
unsealed when specifically requested.

Certain bright doorways don't appear until we're
actually going through them.

It's a field of signs we're invited to read
from the moment of our birth
about the mortal conundrum and immortal solution
of our death.

Our actions imprint on atmospheric celluloid that floats continually
behind us into the
Phantom Archive. When we're
done with our bodies the pictures on that film are
projected on our now-empty corporeal shapes in the air
either for or
against us. The light of the
projector is the beam of God's mercy,
the screen is the stretched silvery
curtain of our hearts.

How much of the world's delight did we savor?
How much Divine Light did we share?
Did our hand refrain from squashing the bothersome mayfly?
Did we open a channel in
the earth for irrigating streams to run free?

Did we see the
dance of sparks in
looping circles around the
heads of our
loved ones?

Did we open a place large enough for the eloquent stranger
to be silent in?

*Did we wave at the train or just
let it mechanically pass us?*

11/6 - 9

## 24 TO WEEP REAL TEARS

And sometimes I wish I could weep with
a gush of tears over the
tops of my lower eyelids for all the
excruciatingly poignant things in this life, let
twin rivers of tears cascade over my lower lids with
small boats in them, for the
point in this life where the
heart is strained to breaking, for
longing, the backed up wells of
frustration, for
utter helplessness when everything seems to
collapse around the
unseen but unscatheable rose tree.

Let tears flow copiously for the darkness we labor under
and those tasty moments when it
breaks and we see the
slope not going up in its
steep and impossible
climb, but smoothly descending,
from the tight little
spigot of the heart most of the
time when it can't quite let those
concentric lake-waters rise
to their natural shores, I would wish to

weep real crocodile tears for my self and the
selves of all others nailed in by the

same slats of lathe, rope-burned by
tensions nearly
inhuman to have to endure,
when a white feather floats down an
air-shaft in winter, when
Thelonious Monk makes his flat fingers ring bells of
cloud-covered temples guarding the
magical scrolls of each moment, when
light pushes stars out the pores of a beautiful face that has
caught the
liquid silver tossed up from below. Weep at the

mention of the secret stairway past our
impassible dilemmas, the sexual
knot finally untied for us all, the
ocean amiable to our touch no less
fierce for its friendliness –
weep for soaring birds, open sky so blue and so often
unscanned by the eyes of
earth-walkers too in a
hurry to fulfill their
monetary obligations and
die.

Weep for the patient shopkeepers, thwarted lovers on
park benches who gaze with unfulfillable
longing at passersby whose figures and gestures,
on no part of their own, spark
fantasies of thunderous
domestic stability instead of
one night stands, when the

heart wishes for nothing but an
assurance so eternal that the whole unfolding
human drama is just a
tiny moment fallen at an
angle in the
kaleidoscope that's placed
lens down on a dark table.

Somehow all our two eyes weep in a huge
accord at once, the power of their
century's old flow enough to level
walls of forgetfulness so ancient even the
ancients couldn't breathe past their heights without
consulting the stars.

To let these eyes wash the world's blackened
windows clean, for the
tragic recurrence of the same old stupidities,
unanimous votes in parliaments and senates to drop
bombs,
maniacs in high places making decisions that mean people might
eat or die,

our tears might flow down our
clothes and drip down our
fingers to the
dark grass that grows at our feet. The floods at our
lower eyelids might
crest and flow, or stay
perched on their lashed edges
forever until we're

cold and dead, when
the whole body weeps, with all its
constituent elements breaking into liquid and
loosening their hold on solidity to sink
deep down into dark brown earth and
weep its
final bodily flood of rich sweetness that we
couldn't weep with our own two eyes in life

  at last.

7/15

## 25  THE FATHER

The father sat back in his stone chair.

Antlers grew on his lap, wasps' nests piled like a
stand of paper basketballs at his left elbow, small
architectural replicas of future cities as well as
ancient archeological sites, pits with amphora handles just
poking out the sides, arranged geometrically
at his right.

In front of him he set a lavish table, not sure if for
the dead who eat only star debris, or for
living guests from his own era to drop by and sample
earth, air, fire and water *hors d'oeuvres* to enrich their
blood and make their
outward selves more transparent.

"*For that,*" he said, sitting back again in his stone chair in the
shape of a giant clamshell, "*is the
purpose of mortal birth: Make the
outward self clear as glass so the
living flame of the inner self can not only
be seen for all its silvery beauty, but also be of
light and heat to those around who might
need it.*" Green

moustaches at least three
miles long grew as he
completed that sentence. His feet

elongated as well, until
terraced rice-paddies
bent white stalks from
green pools between his toes.

Balinese masks fluttered down and filtered out through his face,
Samson's strength rippled up through the
sinews of his back, flew off from
shoulders capable of toppling
pagan temples with the graceful wingspread of
two blue herons, one heading west, one heading east.

Nothing could stop his face from assuming the
grim sculpted beauty of the sphinx in moonlight.
Nothing could stop his
hands from copying out, as if
absentmindedly, all the classically
transmitted texts, their words like
luminous worms opening tiny round mouths to sing, so that the
child of the man can just as openly
listen as they
thrill him to the bone.

The father, normal size now, his
shadow on the wall behind him still
gargantuan, crossed his
ankles, and water trickled out from between them into twin streams.
He cupped his hands in front of his
disappearing face and echoes of millennial prayer down
cloister corridors mingled with

raised vocal chants from
virgin forests, first men and
women on earth singing out into the room for his
open son to hear.

*"We in ourselves are*
*nothing. Hardly*
*even here.*
*Sideways, we're*
*nearly invisible. Each father and son of us only a*
*sound distantly audible in a chambered nautilus, spiraling*
*down to Original Soul.*

*Empty vessel as wide as air set out on its*
*side to catch*

*flood of first light come*
*in from the Source to pour*

*out on the next generation,*
*simple as a bright*

*succession of*
*heartbeats,*

*long as a single*
*life's allotment*

*of breath."*

The father sat back in his chair.

The father became the chair.

7/25

## 26 THE SON

The son sat down in the chair.

*7/25*

PRAYER

Sometimes the whole way is dark,
every curve a naked jaw.
Intricate machinery breaks down,
cogs won't go, straps snap, belts lose hold,
and it seems all the
oiling and greasing we did in better days
has come to nothing. Car broke down. Typewriter broken.
Then a waiting in the heartbeat.

A strange refuge in physicality, eating and
sleeping, washing the
face and hands. The
whole inner being sways back and forth with a
whirring fan, letting it
flow. No
thought, no action. But
where's the wisdom in this?

A dark cave opening in photographic detail – the
maw of the cave could hold a
hairy Gorgon the size of
Texas, or a shy muskrat the size of your
shoe.

*Oh heaven, hold our*

*heads between your*

*blue hands.*

                                                                  7/26

## ABOUT THE AUTHOR

Born in 1940 in Oakland, California, Daniel Abdal-Hayy Moore's first book of poems, *Dawn Visions*, was published by Lawrence Ferlinghetti of City Lights Books, San Francisco, in 1964, and the second in 1972, *Burnt Heart/Ode to the War Dead*. He created and directed *The Floating Lotus Magic Opera Company* in Berkeley, California in the late 60s, and presented two major productions, *The Walls Are Running Blood*, and *Bliss Apocalypse*. He became a Sufi Muslim in 1970, performed the Hajj in 1972, and lived and traveled throughout Morocco, Spain, Algeria and Nigeria, landing in California and publishing *The Desert is the Only Way Out*, and *Chronicles of Akhira* in the early 80s (Zilzal Press). Residing in Philadelphia since 1990, in 1996 he published *The Ramadan Sonnets* (Jusoor/City Lights), and in 2002, *The Blind Beekeeper* (Jusoor/Syracuse University Press). He has been the major editor for a number of works, including *The Burdah* of Shaykh Busiri, translated by Shaykh Hamza Yusuf, and the poetry of Palestinian poet, Mahmoud Darwish, translated by Munir Akash. He is also widely published on the worldwide web: *The American Muslim*, *DeenPort*, and his own website and poetry blog, among others: www.danielmoorepoetry.com, www.ecstaticxchange.wordpress.com. The Ecstatic Exchange Series is bringing out the extensive body of his works of poetry (a complete list of published works on page 2).

POETIC WORKS BY DANIEL ABDAL-HAYY MOORE
Published and Unpublished

**Dawn Visions** (published by City Lights, 1964)
**Burnt Heart/Ode to the War Dead** (published by City Lights, 1972)
**This Body of Black Light Gone Through the Diamond** (printed by Fred Stone, Cambridge, Mass, 1965)
**On The Streets at Night Alone** (1965?)
**All Hail the Surgical Lamp** (1967)
**States of Amazement** (1970)

---

**Abdallah Jones and the Disappearing-Dust Caper** (published by The Ecstatic Exchange/Crescent Series, 2006)
**The Chronicles of Akhira** (1981) (published by Zilzal Press with Typoglyphs by Karl Kempton, 1986)
**Mouloud** (1984) (A Zilzal Press chapbook, 1995)
**Man is the Crown of Creation** (1984)
**The Look of the Lion (The Parabolas of Sight)** (1984)
**The Desert is the Only Way Out** (completed 4/21/84) (Zilzal Press chapbook, 1985)
**Atomic Dance** (1984) (am here books, 1988)
**Outlandish Tales** (1984)
**Awake as Never Before** (12/26/84) (Zilzal Press chapbook, 1993)
**Glorious Intervals** (1/1/85) (Zilzal Press chapbook, ?)
**Long Days on Earth/Book I** (1/28 – 8/30/85)
**Long Days on Earth/Book II** (Hayy Ibn Yaqzan)
**Long Days on Earth/Book III** (1/22/86)
**Long Days on Earth/Book IV** (1986)
**The Ramadan Sonnets (Long Days on Earth/Book V)** (5/9 – 6/11/86) (Published by Jusoor/City Lights Books, 1996) (Republished as **Ramadan Sonnets** by The Ecstatic Exchange, 2005)
**Long Days on Earth/Book VI** (6-8/30/86)
**Holograms** (9/4/86 – 3/26/87)
**History of the World (The Epic of Man's Survival)** (4/7 – 6/18/87)
**Exploratory Odes** (6/25 – 10/18/87)
**The Man at the End of the World** (11/11 – 12/10/87)
**The Perfect Orchestra** (3/30 – 7/25/88)
**Fed from Underground Springs** (7/30 – 11/23/88)
**Ideas of the Heart** (11/27/88 – 5/5/89)
**New Poems** (scattered poems, out of series, from 3/24 – 8/9/89)
**Facing Mecca** (5/16 – 11/11/89)
**A Maddening Disregard for the Passage of Time** (11/17/89 – 5/20/90)
**The Heart Falls in Love with Visions of Perfection** (6/15/90 – 6/2/91)

**Like When You Wave at a Train and the Train Hoots Back at You (Farid's Book)**
 (6/11 – 7/26/91) (Published by The Ecstatic Exchange, 2008)
**Orpheus Meets Morpheus** (8/1/91– 3/14/92)
**The Puzzle** (3/21/92 – 8/17/93)
**The Greater Vehicle** (10/17/93 – 4/30/94)
**A Hundred Little 3-D Pictures** (5/14/94 – 9/11/95)
**The Angel Broadcast** (9/29 – 12/17/95)
**Mecca/Medina Time-Warp** (12/19/95 – 1/6/96) (Published as a Zilzal Press chapbook, 1996)
**Miracle Songs for the Millennium** (1/20 – 10/16/96)
**The Blind Beekeeper** (11/15/96 – 5/30/97) (Published 2002 by Jusoor/Syracuse University Press)
**Chants for the Beauty Feast** (6/3 – 10/28/97)
**Open Doors** (10/29/97 – 5/23/98)
**Salt Prayers** (5/29 – 10/24/98) (Published by The Ecstatic Exchange, 2005)
**Some** (10/25/98 – 4/25/99)
**Flight to Egypt** (5/1 – 5/16/99)
**I Imagine a Lion** (5/21 – 11/15/99)(Published by The Ecstatic Exchange, 2006)
**Millennial Prognostications** (11/25/99 – 2/2/2000)
**The Book of Infinite Beauty** (2/4 – 10/8/2000)
**Blood Songs** (10/9/2000 – 4/3/2001)
**The Music Space** (4/10 – 9/16/2001) (Published by The Ecstatic Exchange, 2007)
**Where Death Goes** (9/20/2001 – 5/1/2002)
**The Flame of Transformation Turns to Light (99 Ghazals Written in English)** (5/14 – 8/21/2002) (Published by The Ecstatic Exchange, 2007)
**Through Rose-Colored Glasses** (7/22/2002 – 1/15/2003) (Published by The Ecstatic Exchange, 2008)
**Psalms for the Broken-Hearted** (1/22 – 5/25/2003) (Published by The Ecstatic Exchange, 2006)
**Hoopoe's Argument** (5/27 – 9/18/03)
**Love is a Letter Burning in a High Wind** (9/21 – 11/6/2003) (Published by The Ecstatic Exchange, 2006)
**Laughing Buddha/Weeping Sufi** (11/7/2003 – 1/10/2004) (Published by The Ecstatic Exchange, 2005)
**Mars and Beyond** (1/20 – 3/29/2004) (Published by The Ecstatic Exchange, 2005)
**Underwater Galaxies** (4/5 – 7/21/2004) (Published by The Ecstatic Exchange, 2007)
**Cooked Oranges** (7/23/2004 – 1/24/2005 (Published by The Ecstatic Exchange, 2007)
**Holiday from the Perfect Crime** (1/25 – 6/11/2005)
**Stories Too Fiery to Sing Too Watery to Whisper** (6/13 – 10/24/2005)
**Coattails of the Saint** (10/26/2005 – 5/10/2006 ) (Published by The Ecstatic Exchange, 2006)
**In the Realm of Neither** (5/14/2006 – 11/12/06)
**Invention of the Wheel** (11/13/06 – 6/10/07)
**The Sound of Geese Over the House** (6/15 – 11/4/07)
**The Fire Eater's Lunchbreak** (11/10/07 –)

www.ingramcontent.com/pod-product-compliance
Lightning Source LLC
Chambersburg PA
CBHW031207090426
42736CB00009B/813